DEDICATION

This book is dedicated to the
students, parents, faculty,
staff, and administrators
with whom I taught and learned
during the 2018-2019 school year.

ISBN: 9798639568831

When PEMDAS was little,
his parents taught him well:
Simplify expressions,
and never chase your tail!

Start at the beginning,
take the steps in order down the path,
remember who you are,
and you'll be doing math!

Parentheses ( )

Exponents a^b

Multiply   c • d

Divide $\dfrac{e}{f}$

Add   g + h

Subtract   i - k

"Math," PEMDAS thought,
"is a silly game to play.

I'd rather kiss my parents 'bye'
and explore outside all day!"

(2 + 1)

=

3

Two parents plus one acorn

Down past the neighbor's garden,
PEMDAS started to run.

"What a big plot they have," he said.
"These vegetables are fun!"

$$(2 + 1)$$
$$\|$$
$$3^2$$
$$\approx$$
$$9$$

A three by three plot

On he went to the meadow,
with the woods coming into view.

"So many flowers," PEMDAS thought,
"for each one I see there are two!"

$$(2 + 1)$$

$$\|$$

$$3^2$$

$$\searrow$$

$$9 \cdot 2 = 18$$

Nine flowers on one side times two sides

Then instead of flowers,
PEMDAS saw lots of trees.

When he started counting,
he added up the plants with ease.

$(2 + 1)$

$=$

3^2

$=$

$9 \bullet 2 = 18$

$+$

12

$=$

30

Eighteen flowers plus twelve trees

At first it was all just fun,
but now the sky grew dark.

PEMDAS looked for the path home,
but he wasn't sure where to start.

"I've simplified expressions,
I followed the steps in order down the path…

Oh!" he cried, "I guess it's time:
I really have to do math."

$$2(2 + 1)^2 + 12$$
$$2(3)^2 + 12$$
$$2(9) + 12$$
$$18 + 12$$
$$30$$

This is how simplifying the expression would look without the story. Can you remember the steps?

"Hello," said a friendly voice above,
"I heard your pitiful wail.

The place you love isn't so far away.
You can get there if you follow your tail."

"I'm SADMEP," said the new-found friend.
"PEMDAS," the young squirrel replied,

"And thank you for the advice, but
my parents said I should never chase my tail,
and I know they've never lied!"

$$\text{S}\text{ubtract} \qquad i - k$$

$$\text{A}\text{dd} \qquad g + h$$

$$\text{D}\text{ivide} \qquad \frac{e}{f}$$

$$\text{M}\text{ultiply} \qquad c \cdot d$$

$$\text{E}\text{xponents} \qquad a^{b}$$

$$\text{P}\text{arentheses} \qquad (\ )$$

"You won't be chasing," SADMEP said,
"just going back the way you came."

"I see now," said PEMDAS,
"the path in order backwards –
we can make it a game!"

$$2(x + 1)^2 + 12 = 30$$

This is how the equation would be presented in
a math class. The "x" is called a variable.
It's also like treasure marked on a map.
Can you solve to find it?

"First subtract the trees you added,

$$2(x + 1)^2 + 12 = 30$$
$$\underline{\qquad\quad -12 \quad -12}$$
$$2(x + 1)^2 \qquad = 18$$

"Then divide the flowers you multiplied."

$$2(x + 1)^2 + 12 = 30$$
$$\underline{\; -12 \quad -12}$$
$$\frac{2(x + 1)^2}{2} \qquad = \frac{18}{2}$$
$$(x + 1)^2 \qquad = 9$$

Undo the multiplication by dividing.
Do you see we're getting closer to having "x" by itself?

"The vegetable garden is a tougher case,"
PEMDAS said. "I simplified by squaring,
NOT by multiplying three times two."

"We have to get to the root, then."
SADMEP knew what to do.

$$2(x + 1)^2 + 12 = 30$$

$$\underline{\qquad\qquad\quad -12 \quad -12}$$

$$\frac{2(x + 1)^2}{2} \qquad = \frac{18}{2}$$

$$\overline{\sqrt{(x + 1)^2} \qquad = \sqrt{9}}$$

$$(x + 1) \qquad = 3$$

Undo the squaring by taking the square root ($\sqrt{\ }$).
When you multiply three by three, you get nine,
so three is the square root of nine.

And there in a happy group were their parents
in the oak.

Both children were so pleased that they could
do the math to find their folks.

They all agreed that the path was tough, and
determination helped them along the way.

There was no need to worry about getting lost
when they played again another day!

$$2(x + 1)^2 + 12 = 30$$

$$\underline{ - 12 \quad -12}$$

$$\frac{2(x + 1)^2}{2} \qquad = \frac{18}{2}$$

$$\sqrt{(x + 1)^2} \qquad = \sqrt{9}$$

$$(x + 1) \qquad = 3$$

$$\underline{ - 1 \qquad\quad - 1}$$

$$x \qquad\qquad = 2$$

Finally, solve what is left in parentheses!
Here, since it's addition, we undo by subtracting.

On Saturday, the new friends ventured out
again, with PEMDAS leading!
Can you simplify the expression to tell where
they ended up?

$$3(3+1)^2 + 10$$

SADMEP took the lead to get out of the woods.
Can you make up a story to go with the steps as
you trace backwards to get them home?

$$3(x + 1)^2 + 10 = 58$$

ABOUT THE AUTHOR

Rachel McNerney is a certified secondary (6-12 grade) math teacher in the state of Louisiana. She earned a Master of Arts in Teaching from Centenary College of Louisiana and a Bachelor of Arts in Philosophy and Languages at the University of New Mexico. She continues to attend workshops on teaching and math curriculum.

Find more resources at MathIsNuts.com.

ACKNOWLEDGMENTS

There are a few specific people I want to acknowledge and thank:

1. My kind and supportive husband, who has encouraged me without hesitation.

2. My dear friend Leigh Camp, who organized the writing retreat that got me to put this idea on paper.

3. My parents, who taught me well.